D0638880

2/11/98

"God never loved me in
    so sweet a way before
'Tis he alone who can
    such blessings send
And when His love would
    new expressions find
He brought thee to me
    and he said
    "Behold a friend" "

                Always -
                Kathy

Gift of Friendship

A COLLECTION OF WARM, BEAUTIFUL

THOUGHTS ABOUT THE LOVE OF

ONE HEART FOR ANOTHER

Compiled by Elisabeth Deane

GIFTS OF GOLD

———

THE PETER PAUPER PRESS, INC.

MOUNT VERNON, NEW YORK

THE only rose without thorns is friendship.

Madeleine de Scudéry

TO MY FRIEND

I love you not only for what you are, but for what I am when I am with you.

I love you not only for what you have made of yourself, but for what you are making of me.

I love you because you have done more than any creed could have done to make me good, and more than any fate could have done to make me happy.

You have done it without a touch, without a word, without a sign.

You have done it by being yourself. Perhaps that is what being a friend means, after all.

Anonymous

Friendship

BLESSED are they who have the gift of making friends for it is one of God's best gifts. It involves many things, but above all, the power of going out of one's self, and appreciating whatever is noble and loving in another.   *Thomas Hughes*

A FRIEND whom you have been gaining during your whole life, you ought not to be displeased with in a moment. A stone is many years becoming a ruby; take care that you do not destroy it in an instant against another stone.   *Saadi*

HONEST men esteem and value nothing so much in this world as a real friend. Such a one is as it were another self, to whom we impart our most secret thoughts, who partakes of our joy, and comforts us in our affliction; add to this, that his company is an everlasting pleasure to us.

Pilpay

❧

FRIENDSHIP is a vase, which, when it is flawed by heat, or violence, or accident, may as well be broken at once; it can never be trusted after. . . . Coarse stones, if they are fractured, may be cemented again; precious ones never.

Walter Savage Landor

❧

IT IS only the great hearted who can be true friends. The mean and cowardly can never know what true friendship means. *Charles Kingsley*

WE CANNOT tell the precise moment when friendship is formed. As in filling a vessel drop by drop, there is at last a drop which makes it run over; so in a series of kindnesses there is at last one which makes the heart run over.

Samuel Johnson

LOVE all, trust a few,
Do wrong to none; be able for thine enemy
Rather in power than use; and keep thy friend
Under thy own life's key.

William Shakespeare

A MAN cannot speak to his son, but as a father; to his wife, but as a husband; to his enemy, but upon terms: whereas a friend may speak, as the case requires, and not as it sorteth with the person.

Francis Bacon

Turn him and see his threads, look if he be
Friend to himself who would be friend to thee.
For that is first requir'd, a man be his own;
But he that's too much that is friend to none.
Then rest, and a friend's value understand,
It is a richer purchase than of land.   *Ben Jonson*

First of all things, for friendship, there must be
that delightful, indefinable state called feeling at
ease with your companion, — the one man, the
one woman out of a multitude who interests you,
who meets your thoughts and tastes.

Julia Duhring

I don't meddle with what my friends believe or
reject, any more than I ask whether they are rich
or poor. I love *them*.   *James Russell Lowell*

8

IF A MAN does not make new acquaintances as he advances through life, he will soon find himself alone. A man, sir, should keep his friendships in constant repair. *Samuel Johnson*

FRIENDS? Yes. Not only friends in flesh,
Not merely friends in time and space;
I want these, but I want as well
The friends of all the human race,
As Lincoln, Shakespeare, Jesus — souls
That make the universe their throne,
And yet from that high seat can stoop
And speak with each of us alone.
St. Clair Adams

FRIENDSHIP renders prosperity more brilliant, while it lightens adversity by sharing it and making its burden common. *Marcus Tullius Cicero*

9

"Stay" is a charming word in a friend's vocabulary.

Amos Bronson Alcott

Something like home that is not home is to be desired; it is found in the house of a friend.

Sir William Temple

O friend, my bosom said,
Through thee alone the sky is arched,
Through thee the rose is red,
All things through thee take nobler form
And look beyond the earth,
And is the mill-round of our fate,
A sun-path in thy worth.
Me too thy nobleness has taught
To master my despair;
The fountains of my hidden life
Are through thy friendship fair.

Ralph Waldo Emerson

TRUE happiness consists not in the multitude of friends, but in their worth and choice.

Ben Jonson

EVERYONE that flatters thee
Is no friend in misery.
Words are easy, like the wind;
Faithful friends are hard to find.
Every man will be thy friend
Whilst thou hast wherewith to spend:
But, if store of crowns be scant,
No man will supply thy want.

Richard Barnfield

NOTHING is more common than to talk of a friend; nothing more difficult than to find one; nothing more rare than to improve by one as we ought.

Robert Hall

A BOOK is a friend; a good book is a good friend. It will talk to you when you want it to talk, and it will keep still when you want it to keep still — and there are not many friends who know enough to do that. A library is a collection of friends. *Lyman Abbott*

ONE FRIEND in a lifetime is much; two are many; three are hardly possible. Friendship needs a certain parallelism of life, a community of thought, a rivalry of aim. . . . Friends are born, not made. Intimates are predestined. *Henry Brooks Adams*

I DO not wish to treat friendships daintily, but with roughest courage. When they are real, they are not glass threads or frost-work, but the solidest thing we know. *Ralph Waldo Emerson*

THE MOST I can do for my friend is simply to be his friend. I have no wealth to bestow on him. If he knows that I am happy in loving him, he will want no other reward. Is not friendship divine in this?   *Henry David Thoreau*

FRIENDSHIP that flows from the heart cannot be frozen by adversity, as the water that flows from the spring cannot congeal in winter.

James Fenimore Cooper

WHO ceases to be a friend, never was one.

Anonymous

THE making of friends, who are real friends, is the best token we have of a man's success in life.

Edward Everett Hale

THE right course is to choose for a friend one who is frank, sociable and sympathetic — that is, one who is likely to be influenced by the same motives as yoursesf — since all these qualities induce to loyalty. . . . Since Happiness is our best and highest aim we must, if we would attain it, give our attention to virtue, without which we can obtain neither friendship nor any other desirable thing. *Marcus Tullius Cicero*

FRIEND is a word of Royal tone
Friend is a Poem all alone.

A Persian Poet

TWO MAY talk and one may hear, but three cannot take part in a conversation of the most sincere and searching sort. *Ralph Waldo Emerson*

14

BE COURTEOUS to all, but intimate with few; and let those few be well tried before you give them your confidence. True friendship is a plant of slow growth, and must undergo and withstand the shocks of adversity before it is entitled to the appellation.   *George Washington*

Do NOT save your loving speeches
For your friends till they are dead;
Do not write them on their tombstones,
Speak them rather now instead.

Anna Cummins

So LONG as we love, we serve. So long as we are loved by others, I would almost say we are indispensible; and no man is useless while he has a friend.   *Robert Louis Stevenson*

No DISTANCE of place or lapse of time can lessen the friendship of those who are thoroughly persuaded of each other's worth.   *Robert Southey*

❧

PURE friendship is something which men of an inferior intellect can never taste.

Jean de La Bruyère

❧

THERE are many moments in friendship, as in love, when silence is beyond words. The faults of our friend may be clear to us, but it is well to seem to shut our eyes to them.

Friendship is usually treated by the majority of mankind as a tough and everlasting thing which will survive all manner of bad treatment. But this is an exceedingly great and foolish error; it may die in an hour of a single unwise word. . . .

Marie Louise de la Ramée (Ouida)

IT IS a good thing to be rich, and a good thing to be strong, but it is a better thing to be beloved of many friends. *Euripides*

THEY that love beyond the world can not be separated by it. Death can not kill what never dies.

... Nor can spirits ever be divided, that love and live in the same divine principle, the root and record, of their friendship.

... Death is but crossing the world as friends do the seas; they live in one another still. ...

This is the comfort of friends, that though they may be said to die, yet their friendship and society are, in the best sense, ever present because immortal. *William Penn*

BE SLOW in choosing a friend, slower, in changing. *Benjamin Franklin*

A FRIEND is a person with whom I may be sincere. Before him, I may think aloud.

Ralph Waldo Emerson

A SLENDER acquaintance with the world must convince every man that actions, not words, are the true criterion of the attachment of friends; and that the most liberal professions of good-will are very far from being the surest marks of it.

George Washington

THE method for the culture of friendship finds its best and briefest summary in the Golden Rule.

Hugh Black

FRIENDSHIP is a word the very sight of which in print makes the heart warm.   *Augustine Birrell*

GREATER love hath no man than this, that a man lay down his life for his friend.   *St. John 15:13*

∾

THE first foundation of friendship is not the power of conferring benefits, but the equality with which they are received, and may be returned.   *Junius*

∾

ARE new friends who are worthy of friendship, to be preferred to old friends? The question is unworthy of a human being, for there should be no surfeit of friendships as there is of other things; and, as in the case of wines that improve with age, the oldest friendships ought to be the most delightful; moreover, the well-known adage is true: "Men must eat many a peck of salt together before the claims of friendship are fulfilled."

Marcus Tullius Cicero

NOTHING makes the earth seem so spacious as to have friends at a distance; they make the latitudes and the longitudes.   *Henry David Thoreau*

ELYSIUM is as far as to
The very nearest room,
If in that room a friend await
Felicity or doom.

Emily Dickinson

UNDER the magnetism of friendship the modest man becomes bold; the shy, confident; the lazy, active; or the impetuous, prudent and peaceful.
William Makepeace Thackeray

THE feeling of friendship is like that of being comfortably filled with roast beef; love, like being enlivened with champagne.   *Samuel Johnson*

"I WOULD go up to the gates of hell with a friend,
Through thick and thin."

The other said, as he bit off a concha's end,
"I would go in."   *John Ernest McCann*

SMALL service is true service while it lasts;
Of friends, however humble, scorn not one;
The daisy, by the shadow that it casts,
Protects the lingering dewdrop from the sun.
                              William Wordsworth

HAPPY is the house that shelters a friend.
                              Ralph Waldo Emerson

TO PRESERVE a friend three things are necessary:
to honor him present, praise him absent, and
assist him in his necessities.   *Italian Proverb*

IN THE life of a young man the most essential thing for happiness is the gift of friendship.

Sir William Osler

❧

TRUE friendship's laws are by this rule express'd,
Welcome the coming, speed the parting guest.

Alexander Pope

❧

A FRIEND is one to whom one may pour out all the contents of one's heart, chaff and grain together, knowing that the gentlest of hands will take and sift it, keep what is worth keeping and with the breath of kindness blow the rest away.

Arabian Proverb

❧

LAUGHTER is not a bad beginning for a friendship, and it is the best ending for one.   *Oscar Wilde*

A MAN's friendships are one of the best measures
of his worth.   *Charles Darwin*

∿

THE wise man seeks a friend in whom are those
qualities which he himself may lack; for thus,
being united, is their friendship the more com-
pletely defended against adversity.

Jeremy Taylor

∿

WHEN true friends meet in adverse hour,
'Tis like a sunbeam through a shower.
A watery way an instant seen,
The darkly closing clouds between.

Sir Walter Scott

∿

THE essence of friendship is entireness, a total
magnanimity and trust.   *Ralph Waldo Emerson*

BUT, after all, the very best thing in good talk, and the thing that helps most, is friendship. How it dissolves the barriers that divide us, and loosens all constraint, and diffuses itself like some fine old cordial through all the veins of life — this feeling that we understand and trust each other, and wish each other heartily well! Everything into which it really comes is good.

Henry Van Dyke

LOVE is a sudden blaze, which soon decays;
Friendship is like the sun's eternal rays;
Not daily benefits exhaust the flame;
It still is giving, and still burns the same.

John Gay

WHEN adversities flow, then love ebbs; but friendship standeth stiffly in storms. *John Lyly*

PEOPLE who have warm friends are healthier and happier than those who have none. A single real friend is a treasure worth more than gold or precious stones. Money can buy many things, good and evil. All the wealth of the world could not buy you a friend or pay you for the loss of one.

C. D. Prentice

FRIENDSHIP hath the skill and observation of the best physician, the diligence and vigilance of the best nurse, and the tenderness and patience of the best mother. *Edward Clarendon*

TRUE happiness is of a retired nature, and an enemy to pomp and noise; it arises, in the first place, from the enjoyment of one's self; and, in the next, from the friendship and conversation of a few select companions. *Joseph Addison*

Do NOT keep the alabaster boxes of your love and tenderness sealed up until your friends are dead. Fill their lives with sweetness. Speak approving cheering words while their ears can hear them and while their hearts can be thrilled by them.

Henry Ward Beecher

THE only reward of virtue is virtue; the only way to have a friend is to be one.

Ralph Waldo Emerson

THE love of friendship should be gratuitous. You ought not to have or to love a friend for what he will give you. If you love him for the reason that he will supply you with money or some other temporal favor, you love the gift rather than him. A friend should be loved freely for himself, and not for anything else.		*St. Augustine*

I WANT not a friend servilely to comply with all my humors and fancies, and ever be obedient to my nod, for my shadow does as much as this, but I want one who will follow me only in obedience to truth, and assist me impartially with his judgment. *Plutarch*

IF A MAN has a friend, what need has he of medicines? *Bhartrihari*

THERE is in friendship something of all relations, and something above them all. It is the golden thread that ties the heart of all the world.

John Evelyn

IF WE would build on a sure foundation in friendship, we must love our friends for *their* sakes rather than for *our* own. *Charlotte Bronte*

THERE is after all something in those trifles that friends bestow upon each other which is an unfailing indication of the place the giver holds in the affections. I would believe that one who preserved a lock of hair, a simple flower, or any trifle of my bestowing, loved me, though no show was made of it, while all the protestations in the world would not win my confidence in one who set no value on such little things.

Trifles they may be; but it is by such that character and disposition are oftenest revealed.

Washington Irving

OF WHAT shall a man be proud, if he is not proud of his friends? *Robert Louis Stevenson*

THE supreme happiness of life is the conviction of being loved for yourself, or, more correctly, being loved in spite of yourself. *Victor Hugo*

Oᴌᴅ friends are the great blessing of one's latter years. Half a word conveys one's meaning. They have a memory of the same events, and have the same mode of thinking. I have young relations that may grow upon me, for my nature is affectionate, but can they grow old friends?

Horace Walpole

Tʜᴇ years between
Have taught me some sweet,
Some bitter lessons, none
Wiser than this — to
Spend in all things else,
But of old friends,
Be most miserly.

James Russell Lowell

A ꜰʀɪᴇɴᴅ is a present you give yourself.

Robert Louis Stevenson

I DESIRE so to conduct the affairs of this administration that if at the end, when I come to lay down the reins of power, I have lost every other friend on earth, I shall at least have one friend left, and that friend shall be down inside of me.

Abraham Lincoln

FLOWERS are lovely; love is flower-like;
Friendship is a sheltering tree;
Oh the joys that came down shower-like;
Of friendship, love, and liberty,
　　Ere I was old!

Samuel Taylor Coleridge

FRIENDSHIP is the allay of our sorrows, the ease of our passions, the discharge of our oppressions, the sanctuary to our calamities, the counsellor of our thoughts, the exercise and improvement of what we meditate. *Jeremy Taylor*

LOVE Him, and keep Him for thy Friend, who, when all go away, will not forsake thee, nor suffer thee to perish at the last.

Thomas A Kempis

ONE of the most beautiful qualities of true friendship is to understand and to be understood.

Seneca

A FRIENDLESS man is like a left hand without a right. *Hebrew Proverb*

WE ARE advertis'd by our loving friends.

William Shakespeare

I FIND friendship to be like wine, raw when new, ripened with age, the true old man's milk and restorative cordial. *Thomas Jefferson*

WHAT do we live for, if it is not to make life less difficult to others? *George Eliot*

❧

IF INSTEAD of a gem, or even a flower, we should cast the gift of rich thought into the heart of a friend, that would be giving as the angels give.

George MacDonald

❧

MY FRIEND peers in on me with merry
Wise face, and though the sky stay dim,
The very light of day, the very
Sun's self comes in with him.

Algernon Charles Swinburne

❧

IF A MAN could mount to Heaven and survey the mighty universe, his admiration of its beauties would be much diminished unless he had some-one to share in his pleasure. *Cicero*

MY FRIENDS are my estate. Forgive me then the avarice to hoard them. They tell me those who were poor early have different views of gold. I don't know how that is. God is not so wary as we, else He would give us no friends, lest we forget Him. *Emily Dickinson*

NOT chance of birth or place has made us friends,
Being oftentimes of different tongues and nations.
But the endeavor for the selfsame ends,
With the same hopes, and fears, and aspirations.
Henry Wadsworth Longfellow

A CROWD is not a company, and faces are but a gallery of pictures, and talk but a tinkling cymbal, where there is no love. *Francis Bacon*

33

A FAITHFUL friend is a true image of the Deity.
Napoleon Bonaparte

FRIENDSHIP improves happiness, and abates misery, by doubling our joy, and dividing our grief.
Joseph Addison

IT IS delightful to me to go mad over a friend restored to me.
Horace

FRIENDSHIP is an education. It draws the friend out of himself and all that is selfish and ignoble in him and leads him to life's higher levels of altruism and sacrifice. Many a man has been saved from a life of frivolity and emptiness to a career of noble service by finding at a critical hour the right kind of friend.
G. D. Prentice

NEW friendships are not to be scorned if they offer hope of bearing fruit, like green shoots of corn that do not disappoint us at harvest time. Yet the old friendships must preserve their own place, for the force of age and habit is very great.

... We must be ever on the search for some persons whom we shall love and who will love us in return. If good will and affection are taken away, every joy is taken from life.

Marcus Tullius Cicero

❧

GO OFTEN to the house of thy friend; for weeds soon choke up the unused path.

Edda [Scandinavian Mythology]

❧

THE comfort of having a friend may be taken away, but not that of having had one.   *Seneca*

My COAT and I live comfortably together. It has assumed all my wrinkles, does not hurt me anywhere, has moulded itself on my deformities, and is complacent to all my movements, and I only feel its presence because it keeps me warm. Old coats and old friends are the same thing.

Victor Hugo

CHOOSE thy friends like thy books, few but choice.

James Howell

HE WHO is true to one friend thus proves himself worthy of many. *Anonymous*

WHEN two friends part they should lock up each other's secrets and exchange keys. The truly noble mind has no resentments. *Diogenes*

THE best preacher is the heart; the best teacher is time; the best book is the world; the best friend is God. *The Talmud*

❧

WE NEVER know the true value of friends. While they live we are too sensitive of their faults: when we have lost them we only see their virtues.

J. C. and A. W. Hare

❧

THE tide of friendship does not rise high on the banks of perfection. Amiable weaknesses and shortcomings are the food of love. It is from the roughness and imperfect breaks in a man that you are able to lay hold of him. . . . My friends are not perfect — no more than I — and so we suit each other admirably. It is one of the charitable dispensations of Providence that perfection is not essential to friendship. *Alexander Smith*

ALL men have their frailties; and whoever looks for a friend without imperfections, will never find what he seeks. We love ourselves notwithstanding our faults, and we ought to love our friends in like manner. *Cyrus*

❧

A TRUE friend unbosoms freely, advises justly, assists readily, adventures boldly, takes all patiently, defends courageously, and continues a friend unchangeably. *William Penn*

❧

IRON sharpeneth iron; so a man sharpeneth the countenance of his friend.

Proverbs XXVII:17

❧

MY FRIEND is one whom I can associate with my choicest thoughts. *Henry David Thoreau*

In making friends, consider well first; and when you are fixed, be true, not wavering by reports, nor deserting in affliction, for that becomes not the good and virtuous. Watch against anger; neither speak nor act in it; for like drunkenness, it makes a man a beast, and throws people into desperate inconveniences. Avoid flatterers for they are thieves in disguise; ... But the virtuous, though poor, love, cherish, and prefer.

William Penn

If THOUGHT unlock her mysteries
If Friendship on me smile,
I walk in marble galleries,
I talk with kings the while.

Ralph Waldo Emerson

LITTLE friends may prove great friends. *Aesop*

I HAVE three chairs in my house: one for solitude, two for friendship, three for company.

Henry David Thoreau

My ONLY sketch, profile, of Heaven is a large blue sky, and larger than the biggest I have seen in June — and in it are my friends — every one of them. *Emily Dickinson*

To BE capable of steady friendship and lasting love, are the two greatest proofs, not only of goodness of heart, but of strength of mind.

William Hazlitt

THE ornament of a house is the friends who frequent it. *Ralph Waldo Emerson*

IF A friend of mine . . . gave a feast, and did not
invite me to it, I should not mind a bit. . . . But
if . . . a friend of mine had a sorrow and refused
to allow me to share it, I should feel it most bitterly. If he shut the doors of the house of mourning
against me, I would move back again and again
and beg to be admitted so that I might share in
what I was entitled to share. If he thought me
unworthy, unfit to weep with him, I should feel
it as the most poignant humiliation. . . .

Oscar Wilde

TWO PERSONS cannot long be friends if they cannot forgive each other's little failings.

Jean de La Bruyère

A FRIENDSHIP will be young after the lapse of half
a century; a passion is old at the end of three
months. *Madame Swetchine*

FRIENDSHIP is the highest degree of perfection in
society.   *Michel de Montaigne*

❧

WE CAN never replace a friend. When a man is
fortunate enough to have several, he finds they
are all different. No one has a double in friendship.   *Johann Schiller*

❧

FAR better 'twere for either to be mute,
Than for to murder friendship by dispute.
                                    Robert Herrick

❧

OINTMENT and perfume rejoice the heart; so doth
the sweetness of a man's friend that cometh of
hearty counsel. Thine own friend and thy father's
friend forsake not.   *Proverbs XXVII:9*

THERE can be no friendship where there is no freedom. Friendship loves a free air, and will not be fenced up in straight and narrow enclosures.

William Penn

THEY only are true friends who think as one.

French Proverb

EVERY true friend is a glimpse of God.

Lucy Larcom

AN ELEGANT sufficiency, content,
Retirement, rural quiet, friendship, books.

James Thomson

THERE is no better looking-glass than an old friend. *Thomas Fuller*

THE GOOD SAMARITAN

A CERTAIN man was going down from Jerusalem to Jericho; and he fell among robbers, which both stripped him and beat him, and departed, leaving him half dead. And by chance a certain priest was going down that way: and when he saw him, he passed by on the other side. But a certain Samaritan, as he journeyed, came where he was: and when he saw him, he was moved with compassion, and came to him, and bound up his wounds, pouring on them oil and wine; and he set him on his own beast, and brought him to an inn, and took care of him. And on the morrow he took out two pence, and gave them to the host, and said, Take care of him; and whatsoever thou spendest more, I, when I come back again, will repay thee. Which of these . . . , thinkest thou, proved neighbor unto him that fell among the robbers? *Gospel of St. Luke*

IT IS a wonderful advantage to a man, in every pursuit or avocation, to secure an adviser in a sensible woman. In woman there is at once a subtle delicacy of tact, and a plain soundness of judgment, which are rarely combined to an equal degree in man. A woman, if she be really your friend, will have a sensitive regard for your character, honor, repute. She will seldom counsel you to do a shabby thing; for a woman friend always desires to be proud of you.

Sir Edward Bulwer-Lytton

KEEP well thy tongue and keep thy friends.

Geoffrey Chaucer

WE INHERIT our relatives and our features and may not escape them; but we can select our clothing and our friends, and let us be careful that both fit us. *Volney Streamer*

I HAVE often thought that as longevity is generally desired, and I believe generally expected, it would be wise to be continually adding to the number of our friends, that the loss of some may be supplied by others. Friendship, "the wine of life," should, like a well-stocked cellar, be thus continually renewed; and it is consolatory to think, that although we can seldom add what will equal the generous first-growths, yet friendship becomes insensibly old in much less time than is commonly imagined, and not many years are required to make it very mellow and pleasant. Warmth will, no doubt, make considerable difference.

James Boswell

THE first foundation of friendship is not the power of conferring benefits, but the equality with which they are received, and may be returned. *Junius*

FOR believe me, in this world, which is ever slipping from under our feet, it is the prerogative of friendship to grow old with one's friends.

Arthur S. Hardy

LIFE is to be fortified by many friendships. To love, and to be loved, is the greatest happiness. If I lived under the burning sun of the equator, it would be pleasure for me to think that there were many human beings on the other side of the world who regarded and respected me; I could not live if I were alone upon the earth, and cut off from the remembrance of my fellow creatures. It is not that a man has occasion often to fall back upon the kindness of his friends; perhaps he may never experience the necessity of doing so; but we are governed by our imaginations, and they stand there as a solid and impregnable bulwark against all the evils of life. *Sydney Smith*

47

IF THOU findest a good man, rise up early in the morning to go to him, and let thy feet wear the steps of his door.   *Ecclesiasticus*

❧

GOD never loved me in so sweet a way before.
'Tis He alone who can such blessings send.
And when His love would new expressions find,
He brought thee to me and He said —
    "Behold a friend."

Anonymous

❧

As gold more splendid from the fire appears;
Thus friendship brightens by the length of years.
                    Thomas Carlyle

❧

THE more we love our friends, the less we flatter them; it is by excusing nothing that pure love shows itself.   *Jean Baptiste Molière*

48

SENTIMENTS are what unites people, opinions what separates them. Sentiments are a simple bond that gathers us together; opinions represent the principle of variety that scatters. The friendships of youth are founded on the former, the cliques of old age are to be blamed on the latter. If we could only realize this early and arrive at a liberal view as regards others in cultivating our own attitude of mind, we would be more conciliatory and try to collect by the bond of sentiment what opinion has dispersed.

Johann Wolfgang von Goethe

FRIENDSHIP maketh daylight in the understanding, out of darkness and confusion of thought.

Francis Bacon

I FIND as I grow older that I love those most whom I loved first.   *Thomas Jefferson*

THE end of friendship is a commerce the most strict and homely that can be joined; more strict than any of which we have experience. It is for aid and comfort through all the relations and passages of life and death. It is fit for serene days, and graceful gifts, and country rambles, but also for rough roads and hard fare, shipwreck, poverty, and persecution. It keeps company with the sallies of the wit and the trances of religion. We are to dignify to each other the daily needs and offices of man's life, and embellish it by courage, wisdom and unity. It should never fall into something usual and settled, but should be alert and inventive, and add rhyme and reason to what was drudgery. *Ralph Waldo Emerson*

THE SONG from beginning to end,
I found again in the heart of a friend.
Henry Wadsworth Longfellow

FRIENDS are the ancient and honorable of the earth. The oldest men did not begin friendship. It is older than Hindustan and the Chinese Empire. How long it has been cultivated, and still it is the staple article! It is a divine league forever struck.   *Henry David Thoreau*

FRIENDSHIP above all ties does bind the heart,
And faith in friendship is the noblest part.
                    Lord Orrery

THOU mayest be sure that he that will in private tell thee of thy faults, is thy friend, for he adventures thy dislike, and doth hazard thy hatred; there are few men that can endure it, every man for the most part delighting in self-praise, which is one of the most universal follies that bewitcheth mankind.   *Sir Walter Raleigh*

TIME draweth wrinkles in a fair face, but addeth fresh colors to a fast friend, which neither heat, nor cold, nor misery, nor place, nor destiny, can alter or diminish. *John Lyly*

❧

A FAITHFUL friend is a strong defense; and he that hath found such a one hath found a treasure. Nothing doth countervail a faithful friend, and his excellency is invaluable. *Proverbs*

❧

WHEN befriended, remember it,
When you befriend, — forget it.
  Benjamin Franklin

❧

No FRIENDSHIP can survive the gift of gold. The generous can indeed forget that they have given, but the grateful can never forget that they have received. *William Henry Smith*

WE TAKE care of our health; we lay up money; we make our roof tight, and our clothing sufficient; but who provides wisely that he shall not be wanting in the best property of all, — friends?

Ralph Waldo Emerson

A PRINCIPAL fruit of friendship is the ease and discharge of the fullness of the heart, which passions of all kinds do cause and induce. We know diseases of stoppings and suffocations are the most dangerous in the body; and it is not much otherwise in the mind: you may take sarza to open the liver, steel to open the spleen, flower of sulphur for the lungs, castoreum for the brain; but no receipt openeth the heart but a true friend, to whom you may impart griefs, joys, fears, hopes, suspicions, counsels, and whatsoever lieth upon the heart to oppress it, in a kind of civil shrift or confession. . . .

Francis Bacon

It is a good and safe rule to sojourn in every place as if you meant to spend your life there, never omitting an opportunity of doing a kindness, or speaking a true word, or making a friend.

John Ruskin

A shallow voice said, bitterly, "New friend!"
As if the old alone were true, and born
Of sudden freak, the new deserved but scorn
And deep distrust....
... The new is older than the old;
And newest friend is oldest friend in this,
That waiting him, we longest grieved to miss
One thing we sought.

Helen Hunt Jackson

When my friends are one-eyed, I look at their profile. *Joseph Joubert*

FRIENDSHIP cheers like a sunbeam; charms like a good story; inspires like a brave leader; binds like a golden chain; guides like a heavenly vision.

Newell D. Hillis

THOUGH friendships differ endless in *degree,*
The *sorts,* methinks, may be reduced to three.
*Ac*quaintance many, and *Con*quaintance few;
But for *In*quaintance I know only two —
The friend I've mourned with, and the maid I
    woo!   *Samuel Taylor Coleridge*

WE are the weakest of spendthrifts if we let one friend drop off through inattention, or let one push away another, or if we hold aloof from one for petty jealousy or heedless roughness. Would you throw away a diamond because it pricked you? One good friend is not to be weighed against all the jewels of the earth.   *Will Carleton*

55

THE language of friendship is not words, but meanings. It is an intelligence above language.

Henry David Thoreau

. . . THE communicating of a man's self to his friend worketh two contrary effects, for it re-doubleth joys, and cutteth griefs in halfs; for there is no man that imparteth his joys to his friend, but he joyeth the more, and no man that impart-eth his griefs to his friend, but he grieveth the less.

Francis Bacon

THE more we love, the better we are; and the greater our friendships are, the dearer we are to God.

Jeremy Taylor

IT IS better to be in chains with friends than in a garden with strangers.

Persian Proverb

THE anxiety of some people to make new friends
is so immense that they never have old ones.

Anonymous

WHEN a Friend deals with a Friend, let the
    bargain be clear and well penn'd,
That they may continue Friends to the End.

Benjamin Franklin

I WOULDN'T give much for the boy 'at grows up
With no friendship subsistin' 'tween him an' a
    pup! *Eugene Field*

I DO then with my friends as I do with my books.
I would have them where I can find them, but
I seldom use them. *Ralph Waldo Emerson*

. . . I HAVE never made an acquaintance since that lasted, or a friendship that answered with any that had not some tincture of the absurd in their characters. . . . I venerate an honest obligation of understanding. The more laughable blunders a man shall commit in your company, the more tests he giveth you that he will not betray or overreach you.   *Charles Lamb*

PROMISES may get friends, but it is performance that must nurse and keep them.

Owen Feltham

THERE are no rules for friendship. It must be left to itself. We cannot force it any more than love.

William Hazlitt

FRIENDSHIP based solely upon gratitude is like a photograph; with time it fades.   *Carmen Sylva*

You mention that you *feel yourself hurt*. Permit me to offer you a maxim, which has thro' life been of use to me and may be so to you in preventing imaginary hurts. It is, always to suppose one's friends *may be right* till one *finds* them wrong; rather than to *suppose them wrong* till one finds them right. You have heard and imagined all that can be said or suppos'd on one side of the question, but not on the other.

Benjamin Franklin

AFFECTION can withstand very severe storms of vigor, but not a long polar frost of indifference.

Sir Walter Scott

IF I mayn't tell you what I feel, what is the use of a friend? *William Makepeace Thackeray*

TRUE friendship is of royal lineage. It is of the same kith and breeding as loyalty and self-forgetting devotion and proceeds upon a higher principle even than they. For loyalty may be blind, and friendship must not be; devotion may sacrifice principles of right choice which friendship must guard with an excellent and watchful care. . . . The object of love is to serve, not to win.

Woodrow Wilson

HE who throws away a friend is as bad as he who throws away his life. *Sophocles*

FRIENDSHIP is like a debt of honor, the moment it is talked of, it loses its real name and assumes the more ungrateful form of obligation. From hence we find that those who regularly undertake to cultivate friendship find ingratitude generally repays their efforts. *Oliver Goldsmith*

FRIENDSHIP is a thing most necessary to life, since without friends no one would choose to live, though possessed of all other advantages.

Aristotle

WHEN friends ask, there is no tomorrow.

Proverb

I WOULD not enter on my list of friends,
(Tho' graced with polish'd manners and fine
   sense
Yet wanting sensibility) the man
Who needlessly sets foot upon a worm.

William Cowper

CONVEY thy love to thy friend, as an arrow to the mark, to stick there; not as a ball against the wall to rebound back to thee. *Francis Quarles*

As you say, we don't need soft skies to make friendship a joy to us. What a heavenly thing it is; "World without end," truly. I grow warm thinking of it, and should glow at the thought if all the glaciers of the Alps were heaped over me! Such friends God has given me in this little life of mine! *Celia Thaxter*

True friends, like ivy and the wall
Both stand together, and together fall.

Thomas Carlyle

Alonso of Aragon was wont to say in commendation of age that age appears to be best in four things; old wood best to burn, old wine to drink, old friends to trust, and old authors to read.

Francis Bacon

THE END